THE AUTHOR, Karen Gemma Brewer, is an award-winning
writer, poet and performer from Ceredigion in west Wales.
Her work combines emotion and mundanity with a strong
sense of the absurd. In addition to her own work she has
edited books by other Wales-based writers.

Dandelion in the Sun

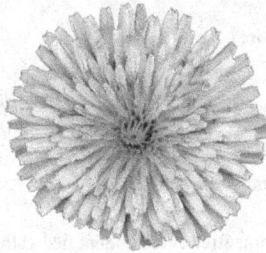

Karen Gemma Brewer

SELECTED POEMS

MOSAÏQUEPRESS

First published in 2025

MOSAÏQUE PRESS
Registered office:
Bank Gallery, High Street
Kenilworth, Warwickshire
CV8 1LY

Series editor: John Eliot

ISBN 978-1-906852-16-0

To Marion,
thank you for your
love and acceptance
not once, but twice

Contents

Introduction

Some poets do not enjoy listening to poetry being read aloud, nor reading their own poetry to an audience. I happen to be one of them. For me, the words were put onto the page and that is where they belong.

Then I met Karen Gemma Brewer.

We were in Romania at the launch of *Currente La Răscruce*, an anthology of poetry in the 'Cross-currents' series, this one featuring poems in English translated into Romanian by the wonderful students of West University of Timişoara with Professor Eliza Filimon. Karen and I could have met up in Wales but we felt it easier to travel halfway across the world.

There was a public reading in a local bookshop in the beautiful city of Timişoara in front of the small but interested audience who typically attend these events. Seated at the front along with Karen and the students who wished to read in public, I wore my serious poet's face waiting my turn to perform. I did, received polite applause, took my seat – and then Karen was introduced. She stood to deliver 'Blind Dogs for the Guides'. I knew and liked the poem. After all, I had chosen it for the anthology. Karen began her poem from memory:

> In the Girl Guides
> I studied just two badges
> Bomb Disposal and
> Rehabilitation of Disabled Pets.

I could see on the faces of the listeners that this wasn't what they expected from a poem. By the end of her reading, I was in tears of laughter. As were others. It's hard to remember whether it was her pitch-perfect delivery, or the words themselves, because Karen is the only poet I know of whose poems are as good as her rendition of them.

The poetry of Karen Gemma Brewer is quite unique. I have come across other 'comic' poets but usually they merely go for the laughter. Karen's poetry is doubled-edged. It can be read and will create a smile without any reference by the reader to the underlying depth.

And there is the catch, the mistake that I am making as I write this. It is too easy to think of Karen as a funny poet. She isn't. To be sure, Karen's performance of her work to an audience is very entertaining. At a festival in Salerno that we attended, she was asked to be the late-night cabaret; requests such as that are rarely made of poets.

Do poets do cabaret? This one does.

Karen's poems are meant to be read from the page, not simply listened to. I believe that in time she will rank alongside the great poets of Wales such as RS Thomas.

The reader will find in these Selected Poems a quality of writing, with a control of language that is very perceptive, and has an appeal to a whole cross-section of readers.

The selection of Karen's poems has been made from across the range of her work. I hope and expect that the reader will see an insight into the mind of the poet, and grow to appreciate and love her work.

John Eliot
Voulmentin, 2025

Blind Dogs for the Guides

In the Girl Guides
I studied just two badges
Bomb Disposal and
Rehabilitation of Disabled Pets.

We practised on dummies,
clipping black and brown wires
inside Bakelite radios,
slipping marbles into eye-sockets
carved in dog-eared turnips,
applying bamboo splints
to fractured rhubarb.

Not 'til the exam
did we see our first live bomb.
I failed that badge.
The following year
it was dropped from the programme
but we did get a new Guide Hut
Christened Nissen
funded from the insurance
and a big black guard dog
we named Clarence
that was only slightly short-sighted.

Lunar Seer

Might I
like the moon
be a daughter of Theia

A circling observer
embraced
beyond arm's length

A wan
minstrel masked
turning laughter from darkness

Luminous creator
quarter
slicing life

Sly draughter of sorrow
exposed
to meteor blows

My dint
erased
at the tide's wash

Moon like

Like the moon?

A Dray at the Beech

Sunburned squirrels sitting on the beech
reach from antique acorn deckchairs
for pre-cut triangular sandwiches
of fish paste, pressed meats, egg and cress.
Buttered slices of bara brith
are dunked in lukewarm tea
cradled in plastic screw top lids
from a glass-lined, tartan tin flask.
Dripping lollies licked in lime and crimson
ice-jar incisors far too ivory.
Nut kin swim in fluffy bikinis
surf on tuffets of foamy sea.

Douglas Fir may be an easier tree to plant
but the broad branches of beech
are a better bet for building sandcastles
where tufted reds squirrel away with buckets
and otherwise redundant, dug-less spades.
Egg-stained greaseproof paper flags flutter
from lolly sticks pricked
into misnamed keeps
that seep the incoming tide
as the sun sets russet on coppery beech
leaves rustle in the breeze and beechwear
hangs drying in their tree.

Condom Conundrum

Shoulder to shoulder back to back
sisters and brothers in a plastic sack
butcher baker candlestick maker
prophet priest catholic quaker
mechanic milkman master of scrolls
defender of honour scorer of goals
robber racist redundant miner
courier carer captain of a liner
red coated huntsman out to kill foxes
smelly inhabitant of old cardboard boxes
winchman hangman judge on the bench
simultaneous translator of french
janitor junkie heroine hag
right honourable member of parliament in drag
banker bitch warlock witch
dictator typist drunk slob
father of evil daughter of god
acrobat on the end of a rope
the man who killed the pope
but not me.

Double Take

Remember you took me
to the tops of the mountains
screaming down valleys
free coitus in a fountain
your stolen licence to thrill?

Today still you shook me
talk of tiling and grouting
vintage steam rallies
free coupons and coach outings
from somewhere over the hill.

Spirit of Life

Ceredigion - grassland, rhos and mountain
Ceredigion - bordered by Teifi and sea
Ceredigion - farming and poetry
Ceredigion - home to the spirit of life

plough the field, spread the lime
sow the seed, return manure
mow the hay, reap the crop
fill the barn, complete the circle
praise the rain, worship the sun
be one with this land

milk the cow, lamb the ewe
collect the eggs, feed the pigs
hang the gate, mend the fence
plant the tree, lay the hedge
train the horse, ride the hill
be one with this land

spot the birds, tickle the trout
see the otter, wink to the fox
pick the mushroom, taste the herbs
crush the apple, enjoy the flowers
count the stars, wave to the moon
be one with this land

Dissident Sausage

Huddled on level four, I shiver to the chill.
Is it night? It is dark and silent,
there is no talking here, only chattering.
It is always dark,
except when the opening door brings a flash of tungsten sun
and we all screw up our eyes and lie still, not breathing,
unified in a single, fearful question,
"Are they coming for me?"

A gust of exhalations greet the thudding eclipse
but the warmth of relief is short lived
and the cold creeps back into my wasted muscles
as I submit to its jolting spasms.
My pink, naked skin is given a blue tinge
and drawn taut across my trembling flesh
by the freezing air.
I am cold, alone and afraid.

There were eight of us.
Then at least we could pool our warmth
but they came for us, one by one 'til only I remain
on level four.
Each instant dawn made sudden enemies of close friends
as all prayed fervently: "That she and not I be taken."
Each thudded dusk turning out a life as well as light.
A saviour of our earthly souls.
Huddled on level four, I shiver to the chill.
A veteran of seven messiahs, waiting for my call.
I hear them coming, how strange?
At every previous blaze of light I locked my lids
and slipped behind my eyes,
in hiding from their white uniformed authority.
Holding up to god a whole register of names
that might be called in place of mine.

But now, now that I know it is my turn,
my eyes are open,
taking in my surroundings for the first time.
I can even smile as I notice,
reflecting in the cold rays,
the two star sign on level five and wonder:
"Who graded this hotel?"

Docile and silent I surrender to their hands.
After all, they have rescued me
from the winter that freezes the mind.
Now I can think again, feel again and I feel warmth.
I am under the spotlight, crowds surround me,
I am prodded and shoved, it is hot, I sweat,
my skin reddens but I no longer fear
my face being read.

What a burden fear is
and how light I feel without it.
No sanction left to still free thought,
I roll and turn in the heat of freedom.
The last bonds loosed
as my skin ruptures.

Life on Marzipan

Yellow planet of almond paste
Holding orbit in outer space
As you circle a golden sun
In the universe of Current Bun

Is this the end of the Bakewell scene
Put your fork through our Stollen dream
Demise of Patisserie too
And all wedding cakes divorcees

As the icing has saddening flaws
Though we've sieved it ten times or more
Like smearing two gooseberry fools
While you ask us to focus on

Nozzles piping dainty rose buds
Oh man, look at that wavy flow
It's the greasiest show
Take a look at that poor man
Icing up the wrong pie
Oh man, wonder if he'll ever know
He's in a nut shelling show
Is there life on Marzipan?

So our economy's tortured now
Always the lowly must draw the plough
Solzhenitsyn turns in his grave
'Cause Lenin's on sale again
Seaborne icing vermillion red
ECT now for all petrol heads
Cruel Britannia still ruled by clowns
Build back better on quagmire grounds

Still the icing has saddening flaws
Party cake in ten tiers ignored
They will write you a writ or ten
Try to force you to focus on

Nozzles piping dainty rose buds
Oh man, look at that wavy flow
Hear the Battenberg blow
Take a look at the poor man
Icing up the wrong pie
Oh man, wonder if he'll ever know
He's in a Bakery show
Is there life on Marzipan?

Giant White Slug

A giant white slug
glistens on the towpath
upstream of the wear between
the footbridge and Shrewsbury Station.

Four inches long
a goddess of molluscs
grey slugs worship at her feet
except there are no feet.

Congregated on every side
some at least are right
and the goddess is not displeased
by pilgrims praying without hands

or knees.

Legless Festivity

Got invited to
the woodworm
Christmas party.

They had sticks
on sausages

Toodle Do's and Don'ts

I tried to grow a Toodle
from the Toodle Pip you sent
but when I added water,
it coughed, and sneezed ……….. and went!

I tracked it down to Paris, France.
Found hiding on a trifle.
But when I arrived to claim my prize,
I was splodged beneath the Eifel.

Clearing cream from off my face
I raced in hot pursuit
Pip still had cherries on its feet
while I wore running boots.

We chased along the riverbank
and as I began to gain,
it dived into the water.
I cried: "Help, a Pip in Seine!"

I leapt onto a river boat:
"Follow that Pip!" my shriek
and as we caught it in a fishing net,
I thought I heard Pip squeak.

But then we heard the squeak again,
sweet and soft and minor,
followed by a mother's yell,
like a foghorn on a liner.

She'd strayed too far,
run too fast, tripped and fallen in.
Her hair was wet, her dress was splashed
and worse, she couldn't swim.

Pip dared to dangle from the net
to grab the drowning daughter
and I dunked both my running boots
to make sure that I caught her.

As we placed the dripping babe
in her grateful mother's lap
a cheering crowd that gathered round
broke out into a clap.

"Hip Hip for Pip," they all proclaimed,
"and also for Pip's friend."
We'd learned when both out of our depth,
on whom we could depend.

The daughter's dad was also glad,
Captain Jean-Marie,
He gave us bread with chocolate in
and tickets for his ferry.

They bumped us up to premiere class,
reclining seats and telly,
the service was: "Oh, so sublime."
Free food and drink and jelly!

The first half of the journey
Pip ate trifle, cakes and stew,
but spent most of the second half
locked in the Toodle loo!

At last we docked in Britain,
returned to our little plot.
But no more thoughts of Toodles,
Pip's one seed I'll never pot!

Lunartrix

Down by the river
there's a wolf at the weir
sniffing the air
smelling your fear.
Will you pay for crossing the Styx?
Two shadows in tune
beneath a raker's moon
howling like Lunartrix
Howling

One foot in a crater
hand on your cheesegrater
phaser set to stun,
prepared for the slaughter
knee deep in the water's
tauter reflection.

Down by the river
two wolves at the weir
one on each bank
motives unclear.
Will you play the old three chord tricks?
Two shadows one tune
beneath a raker's moon
howling like Lunartrix
Howling

True friend or dictator
our alien freighter
invader on the run,
Theia's tide daughter
silver soul-sorter
quartered crescent crumb.

Down by the river
new wolves at the weir
kindred of wild
blind as the seer
blow away the house made of bricks.
One shadow one tune
beneath a raker's moon
howling like Lunartrix
Howling
Howling
Howling
H-O-W-L-L-L-L-L-L-L

Between Us

When
dark cloud gathers in my mind
ten gallon hats of water
hold down my arms
fill the sponges on my feet
and thick mist falls
between the world and me
don't try to hold my hand
or eye
just let me sleep
and smile

Don't Cry for Meat

I don't like cabbage, I don't like swede
spinach sticks in my teeth
I could never survive on vegetarian food
I need muscle
let my teeth attack a carnivorous meal
a very rare steak will do fine
or chicken marinaded in wine.

Don't fry for me cauliflower
give me bacon and eggs for breakfast
slice of black pudding, Cumberland sausage
filleted kipper, liver and onions.

Yes I'll eat Daisy and I'll eat Sam
and Buttercup's baby I feel
will mature into cutlets of very fine veal
and the twin piglets
Christina and Marjorie I will devour
as pork chops, as bacon, as ham
pig's trotters, brawn, pork pies and spam.

You'll die for me Marge and Tina
but the truth is if we didn't eat you
you'd never have been born
have had no existence
if we didn't eat you no-one would breed you.

That puts a charge on us everyone
to ensure your life,
although short
is a good one.

Down the Antiques Market

Down the antiques market
I saw god
walking among
the bric-a-brac stalls

Down the antiques market
I saw god
looking to add
to his collection

Down the antiques market
I saw god
breathing on glass
and rubbing it clear

Down the antiques market
I saw god
haggling the price
of an old universe

Down the antiques market
I saw god
pack a glass orb
in a worn paper sack

Down the antiques market
I saw god
cry over worlds
shattered on the floor

Down the antiques market
I saw god
walking among
the bric-a-brac stalls.

Fly

Refrain:
I'm a fly, I'm a fly, I'm a dirty great fly
with six hairy legs and a compound eye

Overhearing conversations
hanging from your wall
or spitting in your sugar bowl
regurgitating gall

In my acrobatic act
your food are my trapezes
hop and skip from germ to germ
transmitting diseases

I love it in your bathroom
I go jogging around your toilet
then walk across your bread and jam
just before you eat it

Buzzing in and out your ears
dining where your bin goes
cough and sneeze on your baked beans
crapping on your windows

Let you chase me around the room
until you're hot and flustered
fly into your kitchen
leave black footprints on your custard

You take out your aerosol
and spray it at the ozone
cough, cough …
and we both die.

Super View from Top Field

Counting sheep in Top Field
I see Superman fly past
in classic aerodynamic pose;
right fist clenched,
arm outstretched,
legs straight, red cape
billowing behind.

First thought:
'I wonder if there are any left handed superheroes?'
"Don't be silly," I tell myself.
"Superheroes will all be ambidextrous."
Then I wonder what other dexterities
superheroes might possess.

Most obvious is 'Souperdextrous,'
the gravity defying ability to juggle cawl.
Then there's 'Amphidextrous.'
You know, when frog-like webbing
appears between fingers
the instant hands make
contact with water.

That's why superheroes
are rarely seen washing-up,
except those occasions
(and this is how you can tell
if you have a superhero at your dinner party)
when they insist on squeezing
oversized mitts into
your fresh pair of Marigolds.
Some superheroes may be 'Multidextrous'
having the ability
to drink really sweet tea?

87 sheep, 88 sheep, 89 sheep
or should that be 189 sheep?
Baa! I'll have to start again.

One sheep, two sheep, three sheep
oh look, there goes Iron Man – coo-ee!
Looks like he overslept this morning,
little bit of rust.
I wish they'd find a new route to work,
at this rate I'll still be in Top Field
come lunchtime.

I shouldn't be up here at all really
only, my superhero died.
He wasn't doing anything heroic
not even the washing-up.
He'd just come in from seeing to the flock
and was sitting in his favourite chair
waiting for a cup of tea.
When I took it through to him
there he lay
legs straight
arm outstretched,
left fist clenched.

One sheep …....

Relative

My half brother
is propped in the hall
oozing into the wallpaper
by a rack of left shoes
his NHS glasses
dangling.

My step mother
is sitting by the front door
holding a bottle of milk.

At the back door
I see my two faced sister
and wonder
if she is leaving
or entering.

I'm the black sheep
of the family
tangled up in wool.

Thin

Bronzing
bold in a
breath-in
bikini a
breath of
breeze could
flutter high
to fly as a
flimsy
fleeting
ensign
flagging
undressed
distress in
soaring
semaphwoar

Drumming in Your Ears

I'm the sun and you're the earth
you're lost in your own little world
you don't believe the stories of your end
heaven forfend

I'm the earth and you're the sun
you think you got us on the run
but our magnetic field will defend
heaven forfend

You need to get your act together
read my message in your weather
change your ways my planetary friend
heaven forfend

It's our place we're a selfish people
more important that we keep all
our investments on a rising trend
heaven forfend

Can't you see this final warning
feel the force of global warming

We invented nuclear fission
so sure to find a safe solution

If you don't finally stop and listen
you'll be missing from the solar system

It's a fight we're capable of winning
if we keep on talking, keep on spinning

Everybody's leaving it to
someone else to break the news
you never want to hear
in a million years

Everybody's leaving it to
someone else to break the news
you just can't keep
from drumming in your ears

you just can't keep
from drumming in your ears

Village Fool

No-one took any pictures
when they pulled the water tower down
to make way for conversion
of the farm where Granddad worked.
A landmark I always looked for
to tell me I was almost home
and the voices raised in protest?
Just concrete hitting stone.

We were two dozen kids at the village school
learning to live life's golden rules
second, third and fourth generations
believing we could rake the moon.

I hear they filled in Magdelen's Pond
on that sharp bend in the road
where a baby in a sidecar
lays buried under myth and mud.
A haunted, wooded corner
where we children used to play
and the voices raised in protest?
Just sparrows in the maize.

Twenty-four kids at the village school
sold down the river by the Parish Council
who only permit houses
that will sell for two hundred grand.

I may have been your village fool
but I'm sad to see you die.
Locked front doors, curtains drawn,
two cars in every drive.
Nameplates replacing numbers
give a quaint rural address
to collars, ties and shooting sticks
a badge of your success.

Down an old green lane
called Double Ditch
lived an ancient widow
we thought was a witch
and used to double-dare each other
to drink from the standpipe by her door.

Now, it's tarmacked Willow Drive
and the tumble down cottage
looks through double-glazed eyes
on twenty-four seeds from a dandelion clock
drifting on the breeze of a property plot.
Hey lady! What will you bid me for my upbringing?

My roots lie crushed
in a garlic press
on a table
in a green oak kitchen.

Death is Like a Box of Chocolates

Walnut Whipping
Vanilla Evisceration
Butterscotch Stoning
Gas Chamber Cappuccino
Hazelnut Hanging
Lethal Lemon Injection
Keelhauling Caramel
Turkish Decapitation
Black Forest Burning
Strawberry Strychnine
Firing Squad Fudge
Coconut Crucifixion
Passion Fruit Flaying
Guillotine Nougat
Electric Chair Cherry
Coffee Cremation
Blackberry Burial
Death By Chocolate

Just Another Hole in the Head

Through CCTV
zoom in on my name
raise flags of terror
to further your claim
map out my face
record every frame
your bright raisin eye
black hole to my brain
a chip in the block
fishing your game
suck out all emotion
no need to explain
remove all commotion
appearance the same
my escape temporary
won't happen again
forward locomotion
programmably lame
abort every notion
I won't think again
no self-promotion
now all on one plane
value my devotion
new link in your chain

Backspace

Back when there were shops
and people still shook hands
I would drive a white, wheeled car
to a small market town.

Back when food was solid
and vegetables still grew
we'd natter in a café
pay money from a queue.

Back when there was paper
and some of us might vote
we'd write each other stories
pass kisses on our notes.

Back when there was courtship
and hearts still to be won
you tipped my fingers tender
into your open palm.

Back when there was birdsong
and weather that could change
we watched together cling films
beneath our love's sweet reign.

Back when time was counted
and day took turns with night
goose-skin bumped to skin, we slept
in silence not disquiet.

Back when there were children
and death could cheat machines
we promised we would throw the switch
but logged-in to our dreams.

Back then we were human
and thought we'd still be free
down souled to books of faces
in virtual libraries.

Important Questions on Self-Driving Cars

Will dogs still be allowed to ride
with their head out of the window
tongue lolling and lips flapping in the breeze?
Will there have to be a human in the car too?
Will I be permitted to use my phone
or will that be considered a dangerous distraction
from watching television?
Will it have an adolescence regression button
that can be pressed at stop signs
to make loud engine revving
and exhaust popping noises as it pulls away?
Will the bonnet be painted in a sexist resistant finish
that prevents the draping of semi-naked females
even at a car show?
Will it know the way home after dark?
Will it be unable to tail gates or crawl kerbs?
Will it compensate the last remaining manufacturer
of driving gloves?
Will it be able to complete
the London to Brighton vintage car rally
a hundred years from now?
Will the sun roof protect me from solar radiation?
Will it take the long way
when I need to compose my emotions
give myself a pep talk
or hear the end of our song?
Will the vanity mirror tell me who is fairest of all?
Will it go around the block a couple of times
when I am too early
or pull in covertly down the street
when I see their car parked outside your house?
Will it be able to outwit smart motorways
and find refuge in the event of a breakdown?
Will it give me due care and attention?

In Dylan Thomas Summer School Blue

We come from different places
see in varying ways
carry unsuitable cases
act our one actor plays
we hear each other's stories
tell tall tales of our own
white lies and pretences
under cut over blown

Our words span the Atlantic
crash on either shore
phrases thrown like a forest
needle deep on the floor
our lines line-up beside us
stripes that shine with the stars
heart in the heat of a dragon
burnished craft of the Bards

Hillside sheep bleat our star signs in Welsh
destinies tangled in language and fleece
green as the grass stains engrained on our knees
croeso, araf, awen, ysgrifennu

State sidewinder ticks
time's J-crawling trails
hiraeth may hide in your flightcase
Cymru beneath fingernails
barddoniaeth steep your subconscious
Cymraeg's lullaby page
dragon's blood brothers and sisters
lead on each other's stage

Blue water, blue water, blue water
All we see all at sea all we see all our sea.

There Was a River

There was a river
running through here
but now
the bed is dry.

We wasted
all the planet's tears
there are no more
left to cry.

There was a forest
standing on that hill
where birdsong
echoed far.

We cut it down
for direct mail
recovery
for your car.

There was a schoolyard
down the track
where children
staged a strike.

We listened
to their pleas
then did nothing
to put things right.

Crystal
clear waters
evaporate
in memory.

No waterfalls
or kingfisher calls
no kisses
by the sea.

Ten Greenbottles*

You always were too fly for me
but I was pleased to be your toad
'til you tied ten children to my back,
too much for anyone to bear.

Open mouthed demanding babies
killed whatever brain I had.
No space left to breathe or move
their maggot wavings stole my air.

Now I am dust and frozen silent.
Children have all flown my nest.
Nothing left but warts on bones.
A hollow host. An empty chair.

* A variety of greenbottle fly lays its eggs on the body of the common
toad, hatched larvae crawl into the nasal cavity before penetrating the
rest of the head. The toad dies after two or three days and the larvae
eat it, leaving only skin and skeleton.

Nursery Rhyme

Ring a ring of funeral bells
throw the pussies down the wells
ninety people fell and drowned
when London Bridge came falling down.

Ba Ba Black Sheep's locked outside
now the farm's gone apartheid
today's pressures just too much
Humpty Dumpty's cracking up.

Jack Horner rings the Sunday Times
utters a few warning lines
slams down receiver, then he's gone
sticks in a thumb, explodes a bomb.

Sitting drinking ginger ale
Duke of York turns ghostly pale
ten thousand men go up in smoke
their ashes settle around his cloak.

Mary Mary quite contrary
JUMPS! From the eleventh storey
meets the pavement face to face
makes an impact on that place.

Pavement artist then takes part
makes Mary Mary objet d'art
splattered stone stands in the Tate
with Mary Mary on a plate.

Sing a song of 50p
Mummy say one more to me
No more, no more, goodnight, goodnight
God, reaching down, turns off the light.

Mycycle

Tomorrow
I will stand tall
raise arms to the sun
dance in the wind
shelter from rain
nestle with nuthatch and pine martin
rattle with woodpecker
feed squirrel
hide moth
decorate with lichen.

Today
I curl
flesh and bone
an intern
learning to subside
in the entwining
draw of roots
from the sapling
planted
above my head.

Afterthought:
Legacy Circus

The children I leave behind are words
Words that hold my thoughts and dreams
Dreams of love, nightmares of sorrow
Sorrow shared on white in black
Black as tea that's steeped too long
Long shadows strained in shady lines
Lines that catch all fish in rhyme
Rhyme and rhythm, song and tune
Tune into the wavering moon
Moon Boots wading bird to sing
Sing the rhyming fish song worm
Worm into the mind and spirit
Spirit spit that foams the waves
Waves goodbye from alien climes
Climbs the final step to fly
Fly away all lines are cut
Cut and paste away my words
Words the children I leave behind